THE STRATEGY BEHIND SOLVING COMPLEX
PROBLEMS & COMMUNICATING EFFECTIVELY

GENERAL PRINCIPLES OF MANAGEMENT CONSULTING

PAULO MANSO

TABLE OF CONTENTS

Preface 1

1. Introduction to Management Consulting 5
    1.1 What Is Management Consulting? 6
    1.2 Engagement Lifecycle.. 8
    1.3 Feedback Process and Consultant Evaluation 13

2. Problem Structuring & Solving 17
    2.1 Hypothesis-Driven Approach............................. 18
    2.2 MECE 24
    2.3 Issue Tree 28
    2.4 Frameworks... 30
        2.4.1 Profitability Analysis.. 30
        2.4.2 Porter's 5 Forces 31
        2.4.3 SWOT Analysis 33
        2.4.4 Value Chain 34
        2.4.5 Other Frameworks 36
    2.5 Prioritization 38

3. Communication of Key Insights & Recommendations... 41
    3.1 Storyline.. 42
    3.2 Audience 42
    3.3 Deck Structure 43
    3.4 Vertical Logic.. 45
    3.5 Horizontal Logic.. 46
    3.6 Formatting 47

Conclusion and Next Steps 49
About the Author 55

PREFACE

"I apologize for the long letter. I didn't have time to write a short one."

– Blaise Pascal

The goal of this book is to provide an overview of general principles of management consulting. You will learn how consultants operate, how to structure and solve complex problems, and how to effectively communicate your findings and recommendations.

This book is deliberately short. My commitment to you is that we will go straight to the key concepts, without any fillers. It is particularly challenging to read hundreds of pages of business books, so I did my best to condense the learnings from my consulting career into what I believe are the key concepts you should study.

You should find this book useful if you:

- Would like to learn more about the management consulting profession (including if this might be the right career path for you);
- Are a junior analyst looking to establish a solid foundation to your problem-solving skills;
- Are a project manager looking to refine your problem-solving skills and learn new techniques and frameworks;
- Solve business problems at work—whether you are a manager, project manager, or junior resource on a team;
- Are a student interviewing for consulting or other roles that require case interviews;
- Are passionate about learning problem-solving techniques used by the most prestigious management consulting firms.

Throughout the book, you will notice references to "consultants" and "clients." Remember that a client can also be an internal one. Therefore, even if you do not work in a management consulting firm or deliver engagements to other companies, you can still leverage the concepts of this book in the projects you lead or work on in your company. In that case, you are playing the role of a consultant, and whoever you are delivering a project to is your client—it could be your manager, another business unit, an executive committee, etc. Regardless of your role in the team—project manager, specialist, junior analyst, etc.—you can incorporate the general principles of management consulting in your toolbox to become an even better problem solver.

As you read this book, I encourage you to think about projects you have delivered at work recently, and keep in mind the problems you are facing in current projects. Think about how you may benefit from clearly structuring the project and the goal of each phase, utilizing concepts such as the Hypothesis-Driven Approach and tools like the issue tree and business frameworks, and effectively prioritizing and communicating your findings with a proper flow, effective storyline, and objective executive summary.

My hope is that you will find value in the principles covered in this book: from structuring a problem to solving it, and communicating your recommendations in an effective and professional manner.

Thank you for joining me in this journey.

1. INTRODUCTION TO MANAGEMENT CONSULTING

"It takes all the running you can do to keep in the same place."

– Red Queen to Alice[1]

---

[1] The quote refers to the Red Queen's race, an event in the book *Alice Through the Looking-Glass* by Lewis Carroll.

1.1 What Is Management Consulting?

Management consulting is the practice of assisting companies to improve their performance. Management consultants work with clients across different industries and geographies to provide recommendations about challenging problems.

Some examples of clients and engagements are:

- A fintech is looking to expand internationally and wants to prioritize new markets and define its entry strategy.
- An automaker is growing and wants to determine whether to expand its current factory or open a new one in another location (and, if the latter, define which location).
- A restaurant chain had significant losses during the COVID-19 pandemic and needs to decide how many and which units to close across the country to remain profitable.
- Two telecommunication companies are merging and need to identify synergies and new market opportunities with their combined structure.

As you can see, these challenges are extremely broad, complex, and do not have a clear or easy answer. In the next chapter, we will see how to break down such an extensive problem into smaller chunks and structure it effectively to arrive at solid recommendations.

Management consulting is a dynamic, fast paced, and demanding field. It offers fantastic career development opportunities by exposing consultants to interesting (and tough) problems and providing a close look at top management decision-making in major organizations. This opportunity, however, comes at a cost: some consulting firms are notorious for an excruciating work-life balance, mainly due to the long hours worked and amount of travel–pre-COVID-19, a typical project involved spending Monday to Thursday at the client site. The expedited career growth is often fueled by aggressive processes such as the "up or out," when every year consultants are either promoted or fired.

Currently, the main consulting firms are McKinsey & Company, BCG (Boston Consulting Group), and Bain & Company. These firms are often referred to as the Big Three, or MBB based on their initials. Other prominent players in the space include Accenture, Kearney, Oliver Wyman, and Roland Berger.

Over the past decade, the management consulting sector has gone through consolidation. Most notably, the Big Four accounting/audit firms–PwC, Deloitte, KPMG, and Ernst & Young–acquired several prominent consulting firms. For example, PwC acquired Booz & Company (previously Booz Allen Hamilton, now Strategy&) and Deloitte acquired Monitor.

1.2 Engagement Lifecycle

Problem solving is the core of management consulting. The lifecycle of an engagement can be divided into Scoping, Planning, Execution, and Closure.

Scoping: In the Scoping phase, the client engages the consulting firm to help with a specific request. This triggers a series of conversations between the consulting firm and the client to define the project scope. Once the scope is defined, the consulting firm then prices the engagement. Consulting organizations typically have defined billing rates (price per hour) for their resources at different levels, from analysts to partners, and use that to price their projects based on the number of hours expected from each resource over the expected timeline of the project.

As an example, imagine that a company wants to enter a new market in a different country. This client engages a consulting firm to structure a go-to-market plan. The scope discussions are extremely important to define exactly what the company expects from the consultants (e.g., regulatory assessment, opportunity sizing, partnership strategy definition, etc.). Equally as important as what is in the scope is clarifying what is out of scope as well. One of the main challenges consultants face is "scope creep," when the initial scope is not clearly defined and the client pushes for more than what was expected originally by the consultants.

Planning: Once the scope has been agreed upon, a team is assembled to deliver the engagement. The team structure can vary depending on the type or size of the project, but there are typically the following roles:

- Engagement Manager (or Project Manager): Responsible for the day-to-day management of the project, thought leadership, and client relationship.
- Junior Resources (e.g., business analysts): Responsible for the research and analyses, with guidance from the Engagement Manager.
- Principal and/or Partner: Most senior stakeholder on the team; responsible for providing guidance and oversight to the project team and engaging with the most senior stakeholders on the client side. Typically, the Principal and/or Partner would have been involved in the sales discussions from the beginning and would have valuable information to provide the project team.
- Subject Matter Expert: Some projects can be very technical in nature, so there is a need for someone with deep industry expertise. Management consultants are typically generalists until a certain point in their careers, so there might be the need to bring in an expert to support the engagement. Sometimes this role is performed by the Principal or Partner.

Two important steps in the Planning stage are the Pre-Kick-Off alignment and the Project Kick-Off:

- Pre-Kick-Off Alignment: Once the team has been assembled and the resources have been staffed, it is

important that the team who was involved in the sale (e.g., Principal and/or Partner) gets together with the team who will deliver the engagement (e.g., Engagement Manager and other team members). This meeting is essential to review the scope and align internally. Besides discussing key project deliverables and timelines, the team can consider working styles and expectations for career development. The junior team can bring up points that they wish to develop to the Engagement Manager, who can look for opportunities to support their team members. For example, an analyst may have the feedback that they need to improve their communication skills. They can bring this up to their Engagement Manager so he or she can give the analyst opportunities to present whenever possible.
- Project Kick-Off: This is the first formal meeting with the client once the contract has been signed. The goal of the meeting is to review the scope together with the client and agree on key deliverables, timelines, and frequency of touch points.

As a best practice, for the Project Kick-Off, the consulting team would put together a short deck with the following sections:

- Agenda: Slide with points of discussion for the meeting.
- Project Team: Slide with team members and roles on both sides—typically everyone would introduce themselves and their roles at this point.

- Background & Objectives: Slide with more context about the project, including key objectives.
- Approach: Slide with additional details on the methodology/approach that the consulting team will use to address the client challenge.
- Key Deliverables: Slide with clarification about what exactly is being delivered. For example, this could be a PowerPoint deck with the key analyses, summary of recommendations, and roadmap. It could also be an Excel spreadsheet with a financial model, or a Word document depending on what the client needs and what was agreed upon in the scope.
- Timeline: Slide with the different project work streams and how long each is expected to take.
- Next Steps: Slide to mobilize the team. Typically, a cadence of touch points is proposed (e.g., a call with the client once a week). Other items can be discussed as needed. For example, if the team needs data from the client, a data request should be discussed at this point. Another example is stakeholder interviews: it is common for consultants to interview client stakeholders beyond the client project team, so they would need to coordinate this with the client. Best practice is to establish one client resource to be the "project manager" on their side so they can help coordinate agendas, data requests, and any other needs.

Execution: In the Execution phase, the project progresses as discussed in the Kick-Off meeting. Main activities performed during the Execution phase include data gathering, research, in-depth analyses to uncover key insights, translation of those insights into decks, and client presentations / touch points.

It is common for the scope to increase during the engagement, or for some elements of the project to become more difficult than anticipated, so it is important that the project team stays aligned with the client and in constant communication.

Another key aspect of project execution is the tracking of financials versus the budget. In consulting, cost is typically incurred by consultants booking their hours and any other external expenses (e.g., if a third-party is hired, or if there is travel involved). The Engagement Manager is responsible for making sure that the project tracks well regarding its financials (e.g., target margin).

Closure: Once the project is finished, there is a final readout scheduled with the client. Since many projects involve sensible recommendations, a best practice is to schedule separate meetings with each major client stakeholder or decision maker to discuss the key findings and recommendations of the project in advance. While this involves much more work than scheduling a single final presentation with all stakeholders together, it significantly decreases the chance of the final readout going wrong because clients are surprised by the recommendations and disagree with the course of action. The final readout should be almost a formality if the team is sharing their findings with the client as they go and align with each client stakeholder separately to ensure buy-in.

After the final readout, there are typically several adjustments requested by the client, so the team can update the deck after the meeting. The project team also needs to prepare to transfer all knowledge to the client (e.g., decks, Excel models, or anything else that was agreed upon).

When the project is formally closed with the client, a best practice of consulting firms is to sanitize the decks and put together a case study based on what was delivered. These can be extremely useful in proposals and any similar projects that might be delivered in the future.

Consultants are also encouraged to look for follow-on opportunities to support their clients, and to remain in touch with them to build enduring relationships.

1.3 Feedback Process and Consultant Evaluation

Feedback is a fundamental element of the management consulting culture. After each project, the Engagement Manager writes a review for each of their team members. The Engagement Manager is also evaluated—not only by their seniors (e.g., Principals or Partners involved in the project), but also juniors: analysts on the project typically submit upward feedback to the Engagement Manager.

Feedback is compiled throughout projects, and there are generally two major performance review cycles per year, six months apart. These reviews are often referred to as "calibrations." Each team member is discussed in terms of their contributions, strengths, and development areas. The outcome of the review is a development plan that could also lead to a promotion (or lay-off in certain cases).

While the expectations of each level vary significantly, the dimensions by which management consultants are evaluated are the same regardless of whether they are an Intern or a Principal. Consultants are guided by some form of skills or competency matrix. The dimensions and nomenclature differ from firm to firm, but examples of evaluation elements are the following:

Problem Solving: demonstrates excellence in analytics and is able to solve complex problems through thorough analyses, producing error-free work.

Communications: demonstrates outstanding communication skills, both written (e.g., storyboarding and building great decks) and verbal (e.g., in client presentations).

Work Structure & Management: plans and executes work in an efficient and timely manner.

Knowledge Management: assists in creating and curating content that can be an asset to the firm and leveraged in future engagements and proposals.

Client Development: builds solid relationships with clients, develops new and existing clients, manages client relationships, and is perceived as a trusted advisor.

Firm Contributions: contributes to the business besides project work—consultants are encouraged to support broader firm initiatives such as recruiting and training.

Teamwork & Professionalism: works together in teams, demonstrating integrity and professionalism; is open to feedback and coaching.

Even if you do not work at a consulting firm, you can appreciate how these dimensions are relevant to any industry, work environment, or career path. I encourage you to perform a self-assessment on how you think you are doing in each of the dimensions above. Think about what you are doing well and what you could do better in each category and in general. After this reflection, I suggest you ask for feedback—from your manager, team members, peers, and juniors.

Learning about your strengths and development opportunities is critical to the self-improvement process and will help your career in the long run. Some companies do not have a strong feedback culture, so it is up to you to own that process and frequently ask for feedback.

2. PROBLEM STRUCTURING & SOLVING

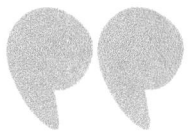

"If I had six hours to chop down a tree, I'd spend the first four of them sharpening my axe." [2]

---

[2] Sometimes attributed to Abraham Lincoln, this quote has other variations, and its origin is uncertain.

2.1 Hypothesis-Driven Approach

The first step in solving a problem is defining it. Based on the available information, consultants should provide their understanding of the situation and validate that they are looking at the right problem before diving deeper into the solving process.

Once the understanding of the situation has been validated, consultants need to structure the client's problem in an effective way. As you saw in the project examples from the previous chapter, the problems can be extremely broad in nature, so we need to break them down into smaller pieces.

The cornerstone of problem solving in management consulting is the Hypothesis-Driven Approach, an effective methodology to structure complex problems. The main benefits of the Hypothesis-Driven Approach are:

- Breaks down the problem into manageable pieces;
- Enables quicker decisions with "enough" data (avoids "boiling the ocean");
- Focuses the analyses with limited resources and time;
- Breaks down the problem-solving process into phases (also allowing the definition of separate work streams, which is particularly important for the team setup so that consultants can work in parallel);
- Ensures systematic coverage of all relevant aspects of the problem;
- Provides a more direct approach to framing the necessary analyses and data gathering.

The Hypothesis-Driven Approach is an iterative process that can be illustrated by the following diagram:

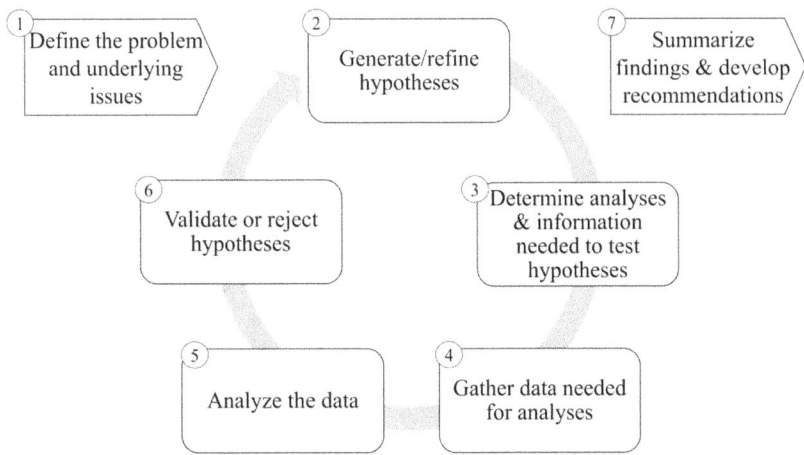

We will take a closer look at each step of this methodology below.

1) Define the problem and underlying issues: Defining the problem should always be the first step. With an understanding of the client situation (e.g., based on the project proposal, scoping discussions with the client, context gathered through research, etc.), this step should allow the team to write down a succinct description of the client's circumstances and a statement about the specific problem they are trying to solve.

Once the problem is clear, it is time to think about the underlying issues. These are the big questions we need to answer to solve the problem, which will provide the initial structure to frame it.

For example, imagine that a company is having a strong turnover issue. Many employees are leaving, and management would like to address this situation.

The problem statement in this case is straightforward and could be something like "The company is facing a turnover issue and would like to increase the retention of its employees."

With this problem statement, we can start thinking about the underlying issues. This involves a brainstorming process. What could be the main issues that drive employees to leave? It could be that competitors are offering higher salaries, or that employees do not see a clear path for growth. Ideally, we would start seeing some patterns among the issues and begin grouping them into the main ones. For simplification purposes, we will assume that the key issues faced by the company that affect retention are *compensation* and *career development*.

Determining the issues is important to ensure comprehensive coverage of the problem and the ability to break it into work streams.

2) Generate/refine hypotheses: Once the main issues of the problem are defined, we start the hypothesis generation process. A hypothesis is a declarative statement of belief that provides an explanation of what is happening. It is like an educated guess. Each issue should have multiple hypotheses, and once we have a good list, we can move on to the analysis phase which will validate or refute each hypothesis.

Going back to our example, we divided our turnover problem into two main issues (compensation and career development). Now we can start generating hypotheses for each of them through a brainstorming process. Here is an example of a few hypotheses:

Compensation Hypotheses

- Employee salary at the company is lower than that offered by competitors.
- Employee benefits are below market standard.

Career Development Hypotheses

- There is no clear career development plan at the company.
- The company prioritizes external candidates over internal ones for more senior roles.
- There is no structured training or development program internally for employees to build skills.

3) Determine analyses & information needed to test hypotheses: Now that we have our hypotheses, the next step is to define what information and analyses are needed to either prove or refute them. For each hypothesis, we will define the analyses that will allow us to confirm or refute it.

For example, our first compensation hypothesis is "Employee salary at the company is lower than that offered by competitors." To validate or refute this, we need to do a benchmark analysis and compare salaries at the company with those of its main competitors. Another example is our first career development hypothesis: "There is no clear career development plan at the company." To check if this is true or not, we would need to look at official company documentation regarding career progression (to be provided by the Human Resources department) and ideally results from an employee survey regarding this topic. This last item could be somewhat achieved by interviewing several stakeholders—personnel from Human Resources to discuss the official company policies, and also several employees to understand their perception of how career development works at the company.

We use this process for each hypothesis.

4) Gather data needed for analyses: At this stage we know all analyses necessary to confirm or refute our hypotheses. The next step is to gather the data necessary to perform the analyses.

In our examples above, salary data would come from the company and market research (for the competitors). We would also request career development policies and any available employee surveys from Human Resources, and take notes from stakeholder interviews into consideration as well.

Note that the process goes from hypothesis to analysis to data, and not the other way around. Sometimes teams request data without having a clear idea of why they need it or how they will use it. The Hypothesis-Driven Approach ensures that the team is clear on what they are trying to investigate/verify (hypothesis) and how they will do it (analysis) before requesting and researching the data.

5) Analyze the data: This step is straightforward—the team works on the analyses needed to verify each hypothesis.

A point worth adding is that hypotheses can be refined based on learnings from the research and/or data analysis. Therefore, this is not a rigid process—it is iterative. New hypotheses can be generated or further refined as the team learns new information.

In our example above, imagine that the team finds out that there is vast documentation about career development available from Human Resources, but survey results demonstrate that employees are not aware of it. Now our "There is no clear career development plan at the company" hypothesis can be refined to "Existing career development plans are not well communicated by the company to its employees." We can now try to validate or refute this refined hypothesis instead, since we learned that there are policies in place.

6) Validate or reject hypotheses: This step is also straightforward. With the analyses done, the team will be able to determine if each hypothesis is true or not.

In our first example, imagine that market research indicated that the company's salaries are indeed below average. We were able to prove the hypothesis and can work on a recommendation based on this fact.

Alternatively, imagine that the company's salaries are on par with or even slightly higher than their competitors'. Our hypothesis would then be refuted. Notice that this learning is just as important as if the hypothesis had been confirmed. The team now knows that this hypothesis is wrong and does not help explain the compensation issue, so they can focus their efforts on investigating other hypotheses.

7) Summarize findings and develop recommendations: Once the iterative process of generating/refining hypotheses, defining analyses and data needs, gathering data, performing analyses and validating/refuting hypotheses is over, the team should be ready to summarize its findings and develop recommendations.

2.2 MECE

When defining the problem you are trying to solve, breaking it down into specific issues is very helpful. One way to do this is to start listing all potential issues that might be related to the problem. Once you have a long list of issues, you can start looking for similarities between them and cluster them into a smaller number of broader issues.

An ideal grouping is **MECE: M**utually **E**xclusive and **C**ollectively **E**xhaustive. This is a fundamental concept in consulting—from defining issues to building an appropriate framework. A MECE approach avoids duplication of effort and ensures complete coverage of the problem. We will take a closer look at what it means.

Mutually Exclusive: Mutually exclusive issues means that there is no overlap between the issues. This guarantees that the team will not be duplicating efforts because parts of the same issue are spread across different work streams in the project.

Example 1 – Pros & Cons:

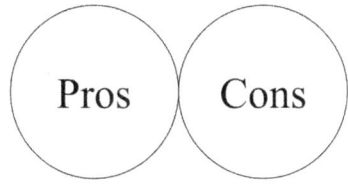

Example 2 – Internal vs External Factors:

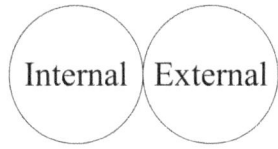

Mutually Exclusive = there is no overlap

In the examples above, there is a clear difference between what is contained in each category. In Example 1, the distinction is between positives and negatives. In Example 2, it is between internal factors (e.g., a company's capabilities) and external factors (e.g., market dynamics).

Now we will look at an example that is not mutually exclusive:

Example 3 – Categories of books:

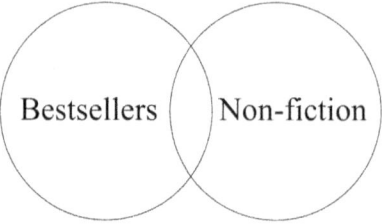

Not **M**utually **E**xclusive = there is overlap

Collectively Exhaustive: Collectively exhaustive means that the sum of all issues provides comprehensive coverage, with no gaps.

Example 4 – Types of transportation:

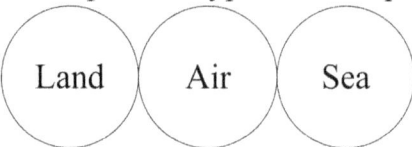

Collectively **E**xhaustive = there is complete coverage

In Example 4 above, we can guarantee complete coverage of types of transportation with the categories land, air, and sea. Therefore, this framework is collectively exhaustive. Notice that it is also mutually exclusive since we can distinguish land transportation (e.g., cars) from air (e.g., planes) and sea (e.g., boats).

Now let us look at an example that is not collectively exhaustive:

Example 5 – Time zone distribution:

Not **C**ollectively **E**xhaustive = something is missing

In Example 5 above, imagine that a company is organized by time zones. We have covered the Western time zones but missed the Eastern ones (Asia Pacific). Therefore, this framework is not complete.

You will notice in the "Frameworks" section that the most common business frameworks are MECE. You should always keep this powerful concept in mind when structuring a problem.

2.3 Issue Tree

The Hypothesis-Driven Approach allows the creation of an issue tree:

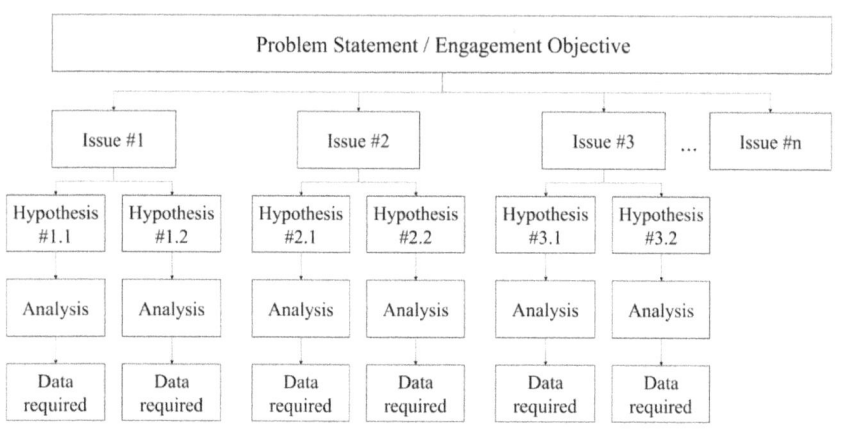

This representation can be helpful to reinforce key characteristics of the hypothesis-driven approach:

- Has a top-down structure, starting with the problem statement or engagement objective;
- Breaks down the problem into smaller, manageable parts (i.e., each issue);
- Provides a MECE framework to the problem to ensure complete coverage while avoiding overlap or duplication of efforts;
- Follows a "hypothesis > analysis > data" flow.

In our previous example, the overarching problem statement is "The company is facing a turnover issue and would like to increase the retention of its employees." The issues are compensation and career development. Each of these issues would be further broken down and explored as a collection of hypotheses, which would in turn trigger analyses, which would require data. An example of that issue tree is:

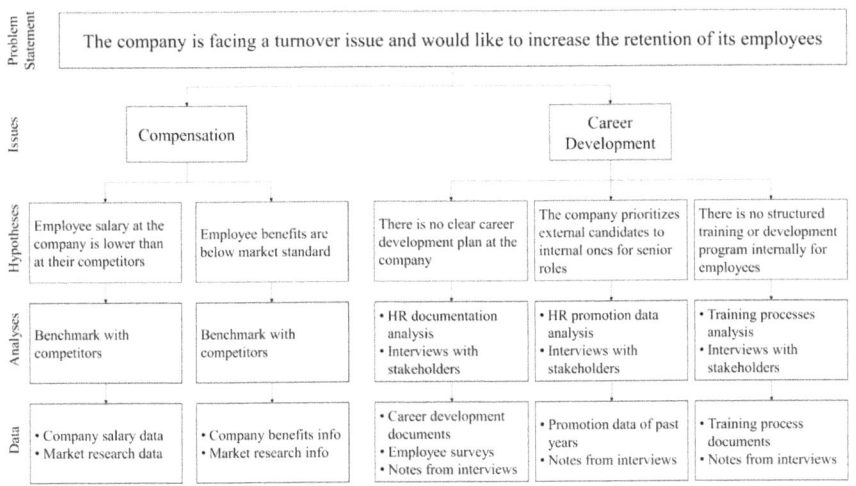

Another way to represent an issue tree is the following:

Issues	Hypotheses	Analyses	Data
	Hypothesis #1	...	...
Issue #1	Hypothesis #2	...	...
	Hypothesis #n	...	...
Issue #2			
Issue #n			

2.4 Frameworks

Frameworks are an extremely important part of the problem-solving process. A framework is a template that structures the problem by breaking it down and guiding its analysis. It should incorporate the key elements that need to be addressed for the problem to be solved, or to provide a satisfactory set of recommendations.

For an illustration of what frameworks are, here are some of the most common business frameworks:

2.4.1 Profitability Analysis

If the problem is related to profitability (of a product or business unit, for example), the simplest way to structure it is by the two components of profit: *revenues* and *costs*. Those two buckets, which are mutually exclusive and collectively exhaustive, can be broken down even further to analyze the root of the situation. For instance, revenues can be divided into *volume* (e.g., number of units sold) and *price per unit*. Costs can be divided into *fixed costs* (e.g., factory rent) and *variable costs* (e.g., cost per unit of production).

This simple framework enables the broader profitability question to be divided into smaller chunks that can be analyzed separately to uncover the core issues.

The profitability tree can be represented as follows:

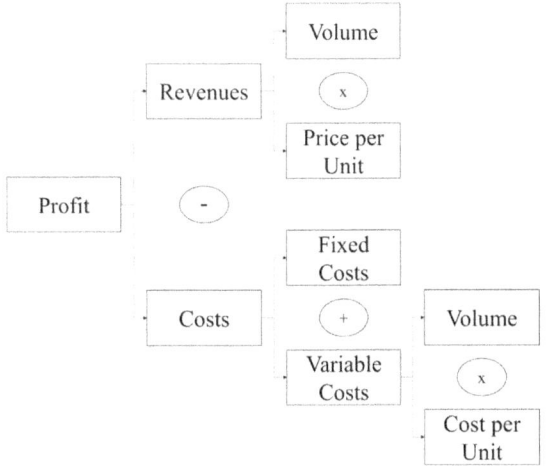

This framework can be useful for business case modeling in Excel.

2.4.2 Porter's 5 Forces

If the problem is related to competition, the Porter's 5 Forces framework is an excellent way to analyze the dynamics of a specific industry and consequently its profitability.

The five forces of the framework represent elements that affect a company's profitability.

Threat of new entrants represents how easy or hard it is for new competitors to enter the space. A segment is more attractive for an incumbent if it has high barriers to entry, which would consequently decrease the threat of new competitors.

Threat of substitutes evaluates the possibility of replacing an incumbent's product with a different one. This dimension is typically evaluated by switching costs (e.g., how costly it is to replace the product), relative performance, and availability of substitute products.

Bargaining power of suppliers measures one side of the production chain. A limited number of suppliers typically means higher costs for the company, since there are only a few alternatives to obtain the necessary inputs.

Bargaining power of buyers measures the other side of the production chain—the ability of customers to pressure the company's price or output. If a company has very few customers (or if they have high price sensitivity), these customers will typically have high bargaining power against the company.

Industry rivalry represents the degree of competition, or difficulty in trying to differentiate from competitors. Industry fragmentation plays a big role in this factor, and if there is little differentiation between competitors' products, there might be a need to spend a significant amount on marketing or innovation, which would impact the company's profitability.

2.4.3 SWOT Analysis

A SWOT analysis provides a comprehensive view of a company's positioning and helps identify core competencies and opportunities while mitigating internal deficiencies and market threats.

SWOT is an acronym for the four dimensions of analysis: **S**trengths, **W**eaknesses, **O**pportunities, and **T**hreats. A SWOT analysis can be represented by the following table:

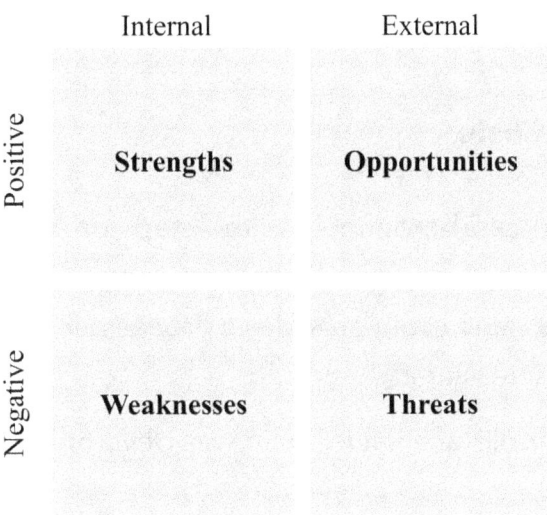

The first two components, *strengths* and *weaknesses*–the first column of the framework above–refer to internal aspects of the company (or product, or business unit) in question. These are things that your company does well and things it could do better. For this internal aspect of the analysis, it is useful to take on different perspectives, such as those of your customer or your competitor.

The other two components, *opportunities* and *threats*, refer to the external environment and should reflect a consolidated view of the opportunities and threats facing your company (or product, or business unit).

Once you analyze these dimensions, you can go a step further and start combining the different quadrants. For example, you can analyze strengths and opportunities together to define which internal strengths your company could leverage to capture certain market opportunities. Similarly, you could define which internal weaknesses should be mitigated to protect against market threats.

2.4.4 Value Chain

A value chain can be defined as the steps or activities that a company needs to perform to deliver a product or service to the market. A value chain provides a process view of an organization or business unit.

A classic example of a value chain was developed by Michael Porter:

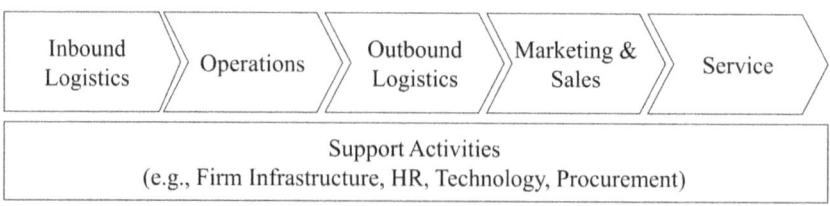

In the example above, *inbound logistics* is the process of arranging materials or parts from suppliers. *Operations* refers to the conversion of inputs (e.g., raw materials) to outputs (e.g., finished goods). *Outbound logistics* is the process of storing and moving the final product to the end user. *Marketing & sales* refers to the process of communicating and delivering the product to customers, and *service* includes all activities that happen after the sale (e.g., maintenance, customer service). This value chain is supported by other activities such as firm infrastructure, human resources, technology, and procurement.

If you were solving a problem related to manufacturing (e.g., consumer goods), the value chain above could be immediately useful to you. However, even if your problem is in a completely different industry, you could still leverage the same concept if the situation involves different, clear, and sequential stages. For example, if your problem is related to the lifecycle of a product, the following value chain would be useful:

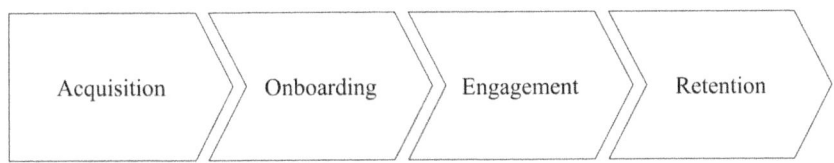

In this example, *acquisition* refers to activities needed to get new customers (e.g., targeting and marketing to prospects). *Onboarding* is the process of teaching a new customer how to use your product once they sign up. *Engagement* focuses on maximizing usage of your product, and *retention* involves developing strategies to keep customers from churning. Note that this lifecycle framework can be used in many different contexts–from a new app to a credit card.

Value chains help divide the problem into distinct, MECE segments and break down the overall problem into smaller parts for analysis.

2.4.5 Other Frameworks

There are dozens of other interesting and useful frameworks out there, such as People / Process / Technology, which helps assess internal capabilities in a structured way, marketing frameworks such as the 3 Cs (Company, Customer, Competition) and 4 Ps (Product, Price, Placement, Promotion), and many others.

Now that we have covered the MECE concept, you will notice that all the previously discussed business frameworks contain mutually exclusive and collectively exhaustive components.

While existing frameworks can be useful in specific situations, there is no "one size fits all" approach. These famous frameworks can serve as a great start depending on the type of problem you are facing, but frameworks should be created– or customized–to address all aspects of the problem at hand.

For example, imagine that your object of analysis is an e-commerce operation. Depending on the problem you are trying to solve, there are many different frameworks you could leverage or create. One example of a comprehensive framework to analyze the entire e-commerce operation could be Marketing / Technology / Operations.

In this example, *marketing* refers to all awareness and customer acquisition campaigns, *technology* encompasses all website infrastructure (both frontend and backend), and *operations* contains all physical aspects of product delivery such as warehousing and logistics.

This provides a MECE way to start brainstorming hypotheses around issues: mutually exclusive because the boundaries of each bucket of the framework are clear (e.g., it is easy to distinguish whether a hypothesis belongs in marketing or technology), and collectively exhaustive because it is possible to address all e-commerce operations with these three elements of marketing, technology, and operations.

Note that you can always tweak a framework to address your specific needs. If you need to be even more comprehensive than the example above, you might consider including "supporting processes" as a fourth category to address invoicing, customer relationship management, and human resources. Alternatively, these could be categorized under *operations* if you want to simplify or if these supporting processes will not be under scrutiny in your analysis.

If you only need to evaluate the actual website, your framework could be focused on the technology piece and consist of different breakdowns, such as frontend and backend, for example.

2.5 Prioritization

As you reach the later stages of your project, you will likely arrive at several different recommendations. Now, not all recommendations are created equal. Some will have much more impact, while others will be easier to implement.

To help prioritize your recommendations, there is a useful 2 x 2 matrix that you can use—the Prioritization Matrix:

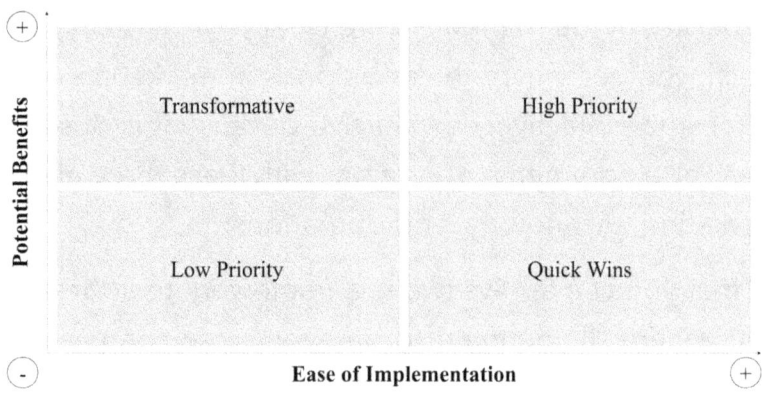

The Prioritization Matrix leverages two axes:

Potential Benefits: This dimension indicates the amount of value that you estimate from your proposed recommendation. You can define "value" differently depending on the situation or recommendation. For example, value could be measured in terms of revenue for a specific scenario, cost savings, time saved, etc.

Ease of Implementation: This axis indicates how easily the recommendation can be implemented. You can define ease of implementation based on different factors, such as time required to implement, number of employees required for implementation, etc.

After assigning your best estimate of potential benefit and ease of implementation to each recommendation, you can plot all of them in this 2 x 2 matrix. Note that the Prioritization Matrix is divided into four quadrants:

Quick Wins: These are the "low-hanging fruits"—recommendations that are easier to implement and provide some value.

High Priority: These recommendations should be the first ones implemented given their high value and ease of implementation. This quadrant of the matrix will likely have very few recommendations since high-value initiatives tend to be harder to implement.

Transformative: This quadrant indicates high-value recommendations that are harder to implement. While typically focused on the long term, these recommendations tend to be highly strategic in nature, which is why this quadrant can be referred to as "transformative."

Low Priority: Initiatives that are low-value and hard to implement are typically deprioritized.

After arriving at your proposed recommendations and prioritizing them using the Prioritization Matrix, you can also put together a high-level implementation roadmap that indicates the proposed order of initiatives, how to sequence them, and estimated time for implementation.

3. COMMUNICATION OF KEY INSIGHTS & RECOMMENDATIONS

"The single biggest problem in communication is the illusion that it has taken place."

– George Bernard Shaw

3.1 Storyline

It does not matter how good your problem-solving process is if you cannot communicate it properly to your client. You may have a very solid analysis, but if the insights and recommendations are not clearly articulated or understood by the client, there is a risk that they will not see that much value in the project. How you tell the story is just as important as the story itself.

Writing should be used as part of your problem-solving process. As you think through the problem you are trying to solve and start going through the Hypothesis-Driven Approach and framework for your analysis, you can already start putting together the story you want to tell. Your deck, like your problem-solving process, is iterative.

It is typically beneficial to start with the end and think about what the final deliverable will look like. You can start writing placeholder headers that tell a story and divide the deck into several chapters according to your problem-solving methodology (one chapter per issue, for example).

3.2 Audience

Always keep in mind who your audience is. During a project, you will likely have to deliver many presentations to different stakeholders. Some of them will be very technical, looking for granularity in your analyses. Others will be more senior and focus on the overall story and recommendations.

When putting together your presentations, start with the objective—of the project, and of that specific meeting.

Then, think about the audience. Put yourself in their shoes. As you read each slide, think about the "so what?" from the perspective of your audience. Is the message clear? Are you providing relevant insights or just describing the analysis? Is each slide relevant to the overarching story—and will your audience care? What question(s) is your audience likely to ask based on what you are presenting?

3.3 Deck Structure

Depending on the complexity of the project, your final deck might be very extensive. Remember that you do not need all the slides to tell the story. Most of them can typically go to an Appendix section at the end—you can always pull them up if there are specific questions.

In general, an effective deck structure should contain the following:

Agenda: Every presentation should contain an agenda slide clarifying what will be covered in the deck and meeting.

Project Background & Objectives: This is a brief reminder of the context of the project in case there are new stakeholders in the room (this can be a single slide).

Executive Summary: The executive summary should provide a good understanding of what was done in the project in a very objective way. Some long presentations will have an executive summary chapter of 5-10 pages that walks through the problem, key insights based on the analyses, recommendations, and next steps. Ideally, you should have a single executive summary page with that information.

You will quickly realize that it is easy to tell a story in 100 pages—you can describe all the work done in extensive detail. However, summarizing months of work into one slide is extremely challenging.

You should view the executive summary slide as one that, even if a client executive leaves the room without listening to the presentation, would give them all the information they need about the context of the project, key findings, and recommendations—not in great detail, of course, but nevertheless, the whole story would be there in just a few sentences or bullet points.

Key Findings: As you develop your chapters in the storyline, you will naturally address the key issues of the problem, the analyses you conducted, and the conclusions at which you arrived.

Recommendations: A presentation is not complete without recommendations. These are actions that you suggest the client take to address the problem in question.

Depending on your audience (especially if it is more senior), you should address the recommendations at the beginning of the presentation to avoid anxiety and questions that disrupt your flow. This is another benefit of the executive summary.

A best practice is to prioritize the recommendations and put together an implementation roadmap. This structured information is much more actionable than a laundry list of actions the client should take.

Next Steps: Just like you should start a meeting with its objectives, you should leave it with clear next steps. If this is an intermediary readout, next steps would be delineating the work that remains to be done or following up on specific action items. For a final readout, they could be discussing implementation support or follow-on opportunities.

It is also recommended to discuss who is responsible for each of the next steps (to ensure accountability) and a proposed timeline for completion.

3.4 Vertical Logic

Vertical logic refers to the relationship of the header of a slide with the content presented on it.

As a best practice, you should avoid using headers that are titles. Titles are fine for slides such as "Agenda" or "Next Steps," but as you go through the main content of your presentation, the headers should be descriptive and summarize the content of the slide.

Imagine that you want to communicate that the GDP of a specific country has been growing at 2% per year over the past five years. Instead of having something generic like "GDP Analysis" as your header, you should write a single, objective sentence that communicates the insight you would like to convey—for example, "Country's GDP has been growing at 2% per year for the past five years." This is much more insightful and already communicates the key takeaway of the slide. A best practice is to have your header occupy two lines at most so it does not take up too much space on the slide. This also forces you to be more objective.

Now, after reading such a header, your client will expect something on the slide that supports that statement. Therefore, an example of content for this slide would be a bar chart with the GDP of the country for each of the last five years, with a trend line indicating its growth (e.g., the CAGR—compound annual growth rate).

This is what the "vertical" of "vertical logic" refers to: content on a slide should support the statement made on the header.

3.5 Horizontal Logic

Horizontal logic refers to the relationship of each slide of your presentation with the previous and the next.

Remember that your deck should tell a story. Therefore, you should structure your deck in such a way that it reads well—it has a start, middle, and finish. Arguments follow each other in a proper flow and the slides are not just presenting random, unrelated ideas.

A great exercise when you are building your presentation is to flip through all the slides and just read the headers (without looking at the content below them). Just by reading the headers alone, you should be able to finish the deck with a clear understanding of what the project was about, the main analyses performed, key takeaways, and recommendations. You should easily understand the story you are telling.

Another good exercise is to start writing the "final" deck as you are going through the Hypothesis-Driven Approach. You can open an empty PowerPoint presentation and start creating slides with just the headers. Those headers will be, for the most part, hypotheses you are trying to validate.

This exercise will allow you to evaluate whether your story flows well and whether your hypotheses give you solid coverage of the problem you are trying to solve.

Another benefit is that, once you have the first version of all (or most of) your headers, you can apply vertical logic to determine the content of each slide—which, as per the Hypothesis-Driven Approach, will indicate the analyses you need to develop to validate the statement on each header.

3.6 Formatting

It is not enough for the deck to *be* right—it must *look* right. This may seem counterintuitive, as the content is the most important part of your presentation, but if the format does not look professional you may lose credibility before the client reads a single word on the page.

General best practices in terms of formatting include:

- Give your presentation a visual identity. This could be the types of visuals or charts you use, colors, font type and size, etc. Consistency is key.
- Avoid too much text on each slide and leverage visuals (e.g., charts, diagrams) as much as possible.
- When using images, make sure they look professional.
- Make sure the content of your slide is aligned and has a consistent format (e.g., type of bullet point, spacing between bullet points and text).
- Indicate the sources of the data you are using for your analyses (e.g., with footnotes). Be clear about where the information you are providing comes from.
- Check for typos.

CONCLUSION AND NEXT STEPS

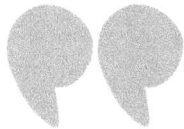

"A journey of a thousand miles begins with a single step."

– Chinese Proverb

Now that you have finished this book, the best way forward is to apply these concepts in practice.

Depending on how familiar (or unfamiliar) you were with the concepts covered in this book, applying some of them might seem daunting. Remember that you can start small, focusing on the things you feel most comfortable with. Maybe it is the Prioritization Matrix, or how to better structure the agenda of the meetings you lead at work.

If you are planning to interview at consulting firms, look for cases to practice and apply your learnings from the "Problem Structuring & Solving" chapter. If you are building a presentation at work, go back to the "Communication of Key Insights & Recommendations" chapter and check if there are best practices you could use to make your presentation even more impactful.

The general principles of management consulting covered in this book are methods and tools that you can carry with you to assist in breaking down problems, solving them, and communicating your insights and recommendations. You can always keep this book handy to revisit some of the concepts in the future. With time, you will build your own repertoire of tools and methodologies to solve the problems you face throughout your career.

My last suggestion—or wish, if you will—is that as you grow in your career, you share what you learn with others, especially more junior team members. As you become more experienced, you have a wonderful opportunity to develop others.

If you have any feedback about this book, please feel free to write me at consulting.author@gmail.com. I welcome any comments or suggestions you may have.

Thank you for reading this book. I am grateful for your time and attention.

"You are where you are today because you stand on somebody's shoulders. And wherever you are heading, you cannot get there by yourself. If you stand on the shoulders of others, you have a reciprocal responsibility to live your life so that others may stand on your shoulders. It is the quid pro quo of life. We exist temporarily through what we take, but we live forever through what we give."

– Vernon Jordan

ABOUT THE AUTHOR

Paulo is a Vice President / Principal at Mastercard Advisors, the consulting division of a global technology company. He is based in Purchase, New York.

In his current role, Paulo is responsible for leading strategic engagements with external clients, supporting the sales of new projects, and developing the consulting team in North America. He also leads a global team focused on artificial intelligence and blockchain. Among his areas of expertise are real-time payments and lifecycle management.

Paulo has been with Mastercard for over seven years, initially based in Brazil. During his time in the company, he has worked on projects for clients in 10+ countries across Latin America, North America, Europe, Africa, and the Middle East.

Prior to Mastercard, Paulo was a management consultant at Booz & Company, working across a diverse set of industries including oil & gas, automotive, telecommunications, and consumer goods. He also worked as an entrepreneur, co-founding and managing a startup in the e-commerce space.

Paulo holds an MBA from Cornell Tech with distinction and a chemical engineering degree from the University of Sao Paulo.

www.ingramcontent.com/pod-product-compliance
Lightning Source LLC
Chambersburg PA
CBHW070853220526
45466CB00005B/1977